THESE AREN'T THE DROIDS YOU'RE LOOKING FOR

A Search-and-Find Book

SCHOLASTIC

Scholastic Children's Books,
Euston House, 24 Eversholt Street,
London NW1 1DB, UK

A division of Scholastic Ltd
London ~ New York ~ Toronto ~ Sydney ~ Auckland
Mexico City ~ New Delhi ~ Hong Kong

This book was first published in the US in 2014 by Scholastic Inc.
Published in the UK by Scholastic Ltd, 2014

HARDBACK EDITION: ISBN 978 1407 14258 6
SCHOLASTIC CLUBS AND FAIRS EDITION: ISBN 978 1407 15249 3

Printed and bound by L.E.G.O., Italy

2 4 6 8 10 9 7 5 3 1

GREAT DANGER, I SENSE! A RUTHLESS BOUNTY HUNTER – THE ASSASSIN DROID IG-88 – IS UP TO SOMETHING EVIL ... FIND HIM, YOU MUST ... BEFORE IT'S TOO LATE!

PODRACERS

If there's a bright centre to the universe, you're on the planet that it's furthest from. But the largest annual podrace in the galaxy is held right here, on Tatooine. Is IG-88 hunting for any of the racers? Find him quickly!

SPOT THE DIFFERENCE

Have you spotted the metal bounty hunter? Well done! Now another task for you, I have.

Yes, *hmmm* ... There are ten differences between this picture and the one on the previous page. Can you find them all?

THE BATTLE OF NABOO

Terrible news! An invasion of Naboo, the Trade Federation has started. The Force tells me that IG-88 is there, too. But whose side is the evil droid on?

Can you find IG-88 in the battlefield?

If found IG-88 you have, look for these, you can:

- a battle droid with a mug
- a Gungan with a rake
- three green, froglike gorgs
- a droid with a beverage tray
- a lost lightsaber
- two droids with newspapers
- a droid with a spanner
- a droid with a road sign
- a droid clinging to a Gungan's leg
- a grey bucket

BOUNTY HUNTER CHASE

Easy it is, to escape pursuit in the busy streets of Coruscant. That's what villains like to think. Anakin Skywalker and Obi-Wan Kenobi are already treading on Zam Wesell's heels.

Can you spot IG-88?

SPOT THE DIFFERENCE

Do you know where IG-88 is hiding? Good!
One day a fine tracker, you will become.

Now look carefully at this picture and find ten tiny
differences from the first image.

THE GEONOSIS ARENA BATTLE

Master Kenobi's secret mission ended up with a fierce battle on Geonosis. Yet, badly outnumbered, the Jedi strike force was. Command the army of clones, I must, to help the Jedi. The sinister IG-88, you must find.

If found IG-88 you have, look for these, you can:

- Master Yoda (myself, that is, yes...)
- Padmé Amidala
- a clone with binoculars
- a Jedi doing her make-up
- Jango Fett
- a big carrot
- a hologram of the Death Star
- a clone tangled in a rope
- C-3PO
- a broom

CATCH GRIEVOUS

Crumbling, the Republic is, under the attacks of the Separatist droid army. Capturing its fiendish leader, General Grievous, may bring an end to fighting. IG-88 is here, on Utapau, too.

To find him, your task is.

If found IG-88 you have, look for these, you can:

- Viceroy Nute Gunray
- an astromech droid
- a pizza delivery man
- two dwarf spider droids
- Chewbacca
- a clone with a camera
- a maintenance man
- General Grievous
- a clone having lunch
- an aerial clone trooper

RISE, DARTH VADER!

Our hope to bring balance to the Force, young Anakin Skywalker was. To the dark side he turned, instead. The evil Emperor is overseeing his transformation into the armour-clad Sith Lord. If IG-88 is there too, find him.

You did it! Yes, *hmmm* ... Are you ready for the next task? This picture differs from the first image in ten tiny details. Use your keen eyes and spot them all, one by one, like the Jedi do.

PIZZA HUT

PIZZA HUT

IN MOS EISLEY

Mos Eisley spaceport on Tatooine – you will never find a more wretched hive of scum and villainy. It seems to be a perfect place to hide for IG-88. Find him, but be cautious. The Imperial agents are everywhere.

SPOT THE DIFFERENCE

Did you spot IG-88? Well done! Now, have a closer look at this picture – it looks the same as the first, but it's not! Can you spot ten small differences between the two images?

ESCAPE FROM THE DEATH STAR

Princess Leia, one of the leaders of the rebellion against the Empire, captured and imprisoned on the Death Star was. While Luke Skywalker is helping her escape to Han Solo's *Millennium Falcon*, find IG-88, you must.

If found IC-88 you have, look for these, you can:

- a stormtrooper taking a photo
- reptilian bounty hunter Bossk
- Obi-Wan Kenobi
- an Imperial TIE fighter pilot
- five mouse droids
- bounty hunter Boba Fett
- an angry grey-haired officer
- a black astromech droid
- Princess Leia
- a black protocol droid

THE BATTLE OF HOTH

Destroyed, the dreaded Death Star has been. Despite this first big victory, in a secret base on Hoth, the Rebels must hide. But the Empire has found them and it strikes back. Is IG-88 on the icy planet, too? Where?

CARBON-FREEZING CHAMBER

In danger the Rebel heroes are! A trap in Cloud City, Vader has set. Captain Solo is about to be frozen in carbonite and traded to Boba Fett. If one bounty hunter's here, then IG-88 must have followed. Find him.

SPOT THE DIFFERENCE

Did you spot the ruthless droid bounty hunter? Good! Carefully at this picture look, now. Ten small differences between this one and the first picture there are.

Can you spot them all?

JABBA'S PALACE

Sold to Jabba the Hutt, Captain Solo was. In an attempt to rescue him, Princess Leia enslaved, has been. Now Luke Skywalker has arrived to free his friends. Did IG-88 follow him? Can you spot the evil droid?

PIZZA HUTT

WANTED

SPOT THE DIFFERENCE

Nothing can hide from young eyes! Found IG-88 quickly, you have. Yes, indeed. *Hmmm* ... As quick will you be, when looking for ten small differences between this picture and the first?

PIZZA HUTT

WANTED

Ready for the final attack on the Imperial battle station – the new Death Star – the Rebel fleet is. But first, deactivate the station's energy shield, a small commando team must. Find IG-88 in case he plans to interrupt the Rebels!

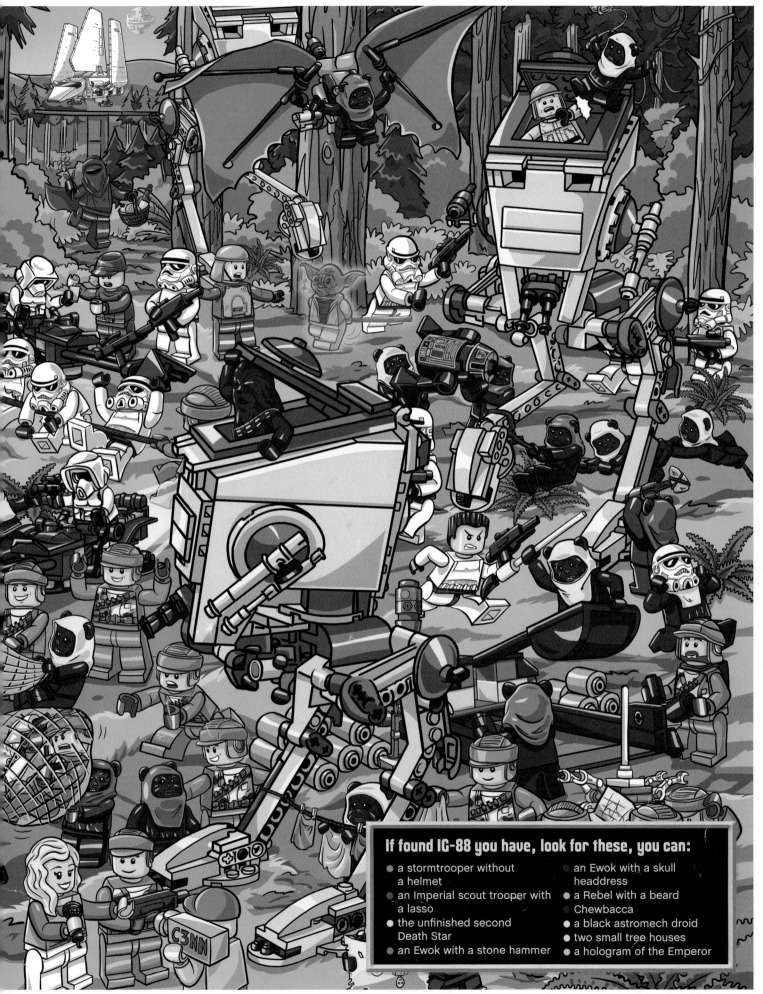

If found IG-88 you have, look for these, you can:

- a stormtrooper without a helmet
- an Imperial scout trooper with a lasso
- the unfinished second Death Star
- an Ewok with a stone hammer
- an Ewok with a skull headdress
- a Rebel with a beard
- Chewbacca
- a black astromech droid
- two small tree houses
- a hologram of the Emperor

ANSWERS

PODRACERS P 4-5

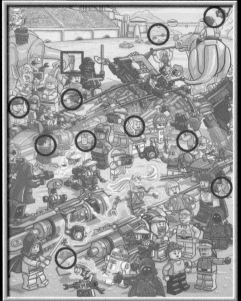

THE BATTLE OF NABOO P 6-7

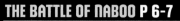

BOUNTY HUNTER CHASE P 8-9

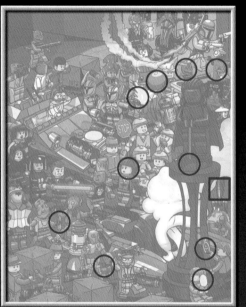

THE GEONOSIS ARENA BATTLE P 10-11

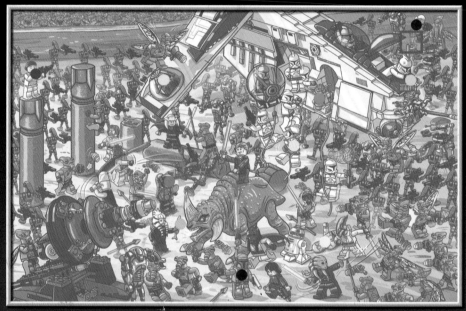

CATCH GRIEVOUS P 12-13

RISE, DARTH VADER! P 14-15

IN MOS EISLEY P 16-17

ESCAPE FROM THE DEATH STAR P 18-19

THE BATTLE OF HOTH P 20-21

CARBON-FREEZING CHAMBER P 22-23

JABBA'S PALACE P 24-25

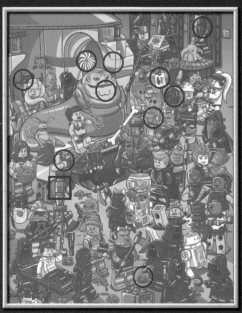

THE BATTLE OF ENDOR P 26-27

DISCOVER MORE LEGO® STAR WARS™ BOOKS!